Publisher: Paco Asensio

Editor: Aurora Cuito

Text: David Hall

Photography: Jordi Miralles

Photographer's assistant: Marta Benach

Art director: Mireia Casanovas Soley

Graphic designer: Emma Termes Parera

2001 © Loft Publications s.l.and HBI,

an imprint of HarperCollins Publishers

D.L.: B-38676-01

Printed in Spain: Anmann Gràfiques. Barcelona

First published in 2001 by LOFT and HBI, an imprint of HarperCollins Publishers

10 East 53rd St. New York, NY 10022-5299

Distributed in the U.S. and Canada by Watson-Guptill Publications

770 Broadway New York, NY 10003-9595

Telephone: (800) 451-1741 or (732) 363-4511 in NJ, AK, HI Fax: (732) 363-0338

Distributed throughout the rest of the world by HarperCollins International

10 East 53rd St. New York, NY 10022-5299 Fax: (212) 207-7654

Editorial Project:

LOFT publications

Domènec 9, 2-2

08012 Barcelona. Spain

Tel.: +34 93 218 30 99

Fax: +34 93 237 00 60

e-mail: loft@loftpublications.com

www.loftpublications.com

If you want to make any suggestions for work to be included in our forthcoming books, please e-mail us at loft@loftpublications.com

Introduction

This book is like a journey, but it is not by any means a travel book. Big as its subject is, it could not pretend to be anything more than a glance at America. The camera, the photographer's eye, catches life where he finds it, the bird on a limb an instant before it is gone. This book then, is a kind of mosaic of diverse, contrasting glimpses, images that come together to tell a story that could not be told in any other way.

Our story, like all stories, is based on certain suppositions. We suppose that a nation is made up of landscape and people and that its history consists in great part of how each of these shaped and transformed the other. And we take architecture as the product of this meeting of man and landscape, as the way people make their own place in the landscape, in shapes and structures that not only serve to shelter from rain and wind and cold but also make statements about who they are or who they think they are.

This is not a history book, though there is history in it. There is history, evidently, in Jefferson's house at Monticello, in the old Boston churches and mansions of the old South, a different sort of histo-

ry in the pottery and weaving of the Indians of the Southwest with their traditional designs passed down over the centuries. And there is yet another, more profound history to be found in the trees and rocks, in mountain ranges and the vast emptiness of the great deserts.

When the first Europeans arrived in what is now the United States, one great forest extended from the Atlantic Ocean to the banks of the Mississippi. Only a few traces of that mighty woodland remain, but a quiet walk in Shenandoah National Park in northern Virginia or a hike in Vermont's Green Mountains plus a little imagination can take us back to that time, before the forests were felled to build our towns and cities and create our farmland.

It has been said that travelers are always looking for the past - their own or someone else's - which is why tourists in Europe, whatever their religious beliefs, spend so much time poking their noses into gloomy medieval churches. In America, the past the traveler goes out looking for is the past of a land before man put his hand to it, the primeval swamp of the Everglades, where a small band of Seminole Indians held out against

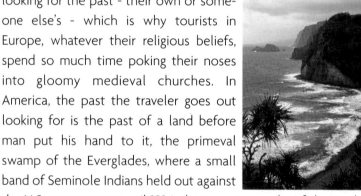

the U.S. government until 1934, the towering peaks of the Rockies, still home to the grizzly and the bald eagle, the bone-dry desert lands of the Southwest and the great Sequoia forests. American history is the story of the taming of the wilderness, and the only

way to really get in touch with that history is to experience one of those places where the wilderness still remains untamed.

The swift, inexorable, colossal expansion to the west in the 19th century of what was at the beginning of that century a little country clinging to the Atlantic coast left its mark on the American character, forging a brash, daring, adventurous people, with a tremendous confidence in their own skills and luck.

The expansion left its mark on the landscape too. It was not just explorers, Indian fighters, buffalo hunters, cowboys and cavalry scouts that tamed the wilderness, but also the railroads and highways laid out across it,

and the towns and cities that sprung up at their junctions and crossroads. The city carves out its space on the landscape and becomes in turn a kind of landscape of its own, with its skyscrapers and subways, its streets and neighborhoods, its buildings that spring up and grow old, pages of history in themselves. A landscape that is intricate and artificial, tense and dynamic, constantly changing.

"There are a million stories in the city," a now long forgotten television series used to begin, while the camera panned row upon row of grimly anonymous city buildings, "and this is one of them." In this book those stories are to be found in faces and gestures, peo-

ple, not just from the city, but also from suburbs, small country towns. The camera captures the fleeting, irretrievable moment - life on the run - and holds it still. Every picture

tells a story, they say, in the wrinkles on a face, the way a hand rests on a table, the posture of a body in repose. And all these faces, with their different colors and shapes, each one a story in itself, are at the same time, taken together, the history of a people.

The first Americans were, of course, the native Americans, or Indians. The first Europeans to arrive were the Spaniards, then came the English, then the Dutch who founded New Amsterdam, later named New York after and African Americans whowhere brought as slaves to work the fields of the South. As the nation grew there came Germans, Norwegians, Swedes, Jews from Russia, Ukrai-

nians, Poles, Bohemians, Irish, Italians, Greeks and Chinese that worked to build the railroad. Today there are Americans from just about every place in the world. A million stories, a mosaic, a tapestry of stories.

The explosion of energy that was the America of the 19th century - not only the westward expansion but also the rise of industry, the railroads, steel, the country's consolidation as an economic power - left a heritage in the form of a dynamic, restless vitality that shows no signs of abating as we enter upon the 21st. But it has to a great extent changed direction. The Puritan philosophy, the famous Protestant ethic of hard work, prayer and no fun is for most Americans today a quaint historical memory but not, by any means, a way of life. In the 20th century the same enterprising spirit that

created the assembly line, invented and mass produced the airplane and built the spacecraft that put the first men on the moon, also created the movies and made a little suburb of Los Angeles with the bucolic name of Hollywood, the undisputed capital of what we now call the entertainment industry. Very early on in the century, smart entrepreneurs saw the leisure society just around the corner and put their money on it.

The America of today is a hedonistic, consumer society that would no doubt scandalize the Pilgrim Fathers. But Americans still work hard, and today they bring the same boundless energy that built the nation to enjoying their leisure. Americans work hard at having fun. No country in the world is as sports minded as the United States, where the three major sports, baseball, basketball and football, were invented and where the

sports industry, with everything from hockey match tickets to skating shorts, racing cars to baseball mitts, represents billions of dollars a year. And along with sports we have hobbies, social life, gardening, cultural events, travel...

America is still a country on the move. In no other country in the world do people change their place of residence as frequently as Americans do, and the lure of the open road, already an American

tradition i when Huckleberry Finn was young, has made America a country on wheels. Nobody loves their cars quite like Americans do, and the mighty gas-guzzlers of the fifties, with their

flamboyant chrome and fins like fighter plane wings, were symbols of a love affair gone wild.

The United States today is a pluralistic, open, adventurous society with an apparently boundless curiosity and enthusiasm. In time, the irrepressible consumerism of the postwar period gave way to a more sophisticated concern for what we call quality of life, a concept which inevitably involves a respect for the environment, a recognition of the need for a harmonious relationship between human beings and the landscape in which they live.

The story of American architecture is the story of a growing self-awareness. The buildings of colonial times, when not simply meeting the needs presented by climate and terrain, faithfully followed European models. Truly American architectural style began with independence, with the Greek Revival and Federalist styles that underscored the idea that the new nation was founded on the principles of classical antiquity. The 19th century saw grandiose public and commercial buildings, often extravagant homes in a variety of ornate, Victorian styles. The

close of the century brought with it the first skyscrapers, perhaps the most eloquent symbol of the audacity and vigor of the American spirit, and with them the beginning of what we know as modern architecture. A volatile, growing society with a passion for change and experiment made the American city the ideal stage for the bold, Promethean feats of modern architecture, gleaming artifacts of steel and glass that dared to reach for the sky and ingeniously learned to bend with the winds. While architecture for the home, on a quieter, human scale and in tune with the sensibility of the times, works with an esthetic of simplicity, space and light. Man and technology are finding their place in a landscape that we are resolved to respect and conserve.

The first European settlers in North America found themselves on the edge of a continent so vast and unknown that it must at times have seemed about to swallow them up. And sometimes it did. The first English colony, for example, was founded on Roanoke Island, North Carolina, in 1587. The colonists' leader, John White, returned to England to procure supplies and when he arrived back in 1590, having been delayed by the Spanish Armada, he found that the entire colony, about 100 souls, had vanished, leaving only the enigmatic letters, "CROATOAN" carved on a tree. No one has ever been able to figure out where they went, or why.

No doubt there was much that was daunting about the new land, and was much different then. Dense tangled forests covered the eastern seaboard full of a variety of animal species, most of which the newcomers had never seen before. Almost three hundred years after the first Europeans set foot on what eventually became the United States of America most of the population was still concentrated in a relatively narrow band down the Atlantic coast. Even there the contrasts were staggering, from Florida with its glistening beaches and fourteen-foot crocodiles in the Everglades to New England's stormy shores and bitterly cold, snowbound winters.

The English peopled most of that Atlantic coast, while Spaniards settled in the balmier climes of Florida and California and the French came down the St. Lawrence River from the north, exploring the Great Lakes and traveling down the Mississippi. Most of the vast area from the colonies along the Atlantic to the Pacific coast was little known except to handfuls of explorers, hunters and trappers, men drawn by the peculiar attraction of the mystery, solitude and danger of the wilderness.

In 1803 American envoys sent to negotiate a grant of free access to the Mississippi River from the French and to try to buy the booming port of New Orleans were amazed to hear that the Emperor Napoleon, in need of money for an immanent war with England, was ready to sell all of the French territory in North America, from the Mississippi River to the Rockies and from Canada to the Gulf of Mexico. The Louisiana Purchase turned out to be the best land deal in U.S. history, 828,000 square miles for $15 million, about 3 cents an acre.

Landscape

Hardly anyone, least of all Napoleon, who had other things on his mind, had much of an idea about what was there. But they soon found out. The headwaters of the Missouri, the Black Hills, the Great Plains, teeming with thundering herds of buffalo. A sea of grass that in less than a century would turn into mile after mile of corn and wheat fields.

On the other side of the plains stood the Rocky Mountains, young mountains the geologists tell us, since they are only about 70 million years old, sharp snow-capped peaks that form the Continental Divide, the waters flowing down the eastern slopes going into the Atlantic or the Gulf of Mexico and those on the west into the Pacific. It is here that great rivers like the Missouri, the Rio Grande, the Colorado and the Columbia get their start.

The American Southwest is home to the great American deserts, harsh and weirdly beautiful. Across the desert is California, with its mild climate, breathtaking coastline and majestic redwood forests, a sort of Promised Land. Wagon trains of settlers from the East were already heading for what was still the Mexican province of California in the 1840s, but it was the discovery of gold near what is now Sacramento in 1849 that brought the first massive influx of population, starting a trend that has not stopped since. In the early part of the 20th century the California sun and the proximity of dramatic scenery in which to recreate everything from Indian wars to the flight of the Israelites out of Egypt made Hollywood a natural capital for a movie industry still in swaddling clothes. Even today the combination of climate, natural beauty and economic opportunity makes California a magnet for restless ambitions, making it the most dynamic state in the union.

The growth of the Pacific Northwest was much less spectacular, and as a result much of its particular natural beauty, its mountains, deep evergreen forests and rainy coasts, has remained relatively unspoiled.

The contrasting landscapes across the great sweep of the continental United States left their mark on the way of life and character of its people. The taciturn, hard-working New Englander, the slow-talking, hospitable people of the South, the steady, easy-going Midwesterner, the rugged, resourceful, individualist of the West and the cool, cosmopolitan Californian are all perhaps clichés in today's rapidly changing world, yet still serve to remind us how the land helps to shape the people who live on it.

Landscape

Cities

On October 8, 1871, fire broke out in the O'Leary barn, supposedly caused by Mrs. O'Leary's cow kicking over a lamp, and thus began the Great Chicago Fire, which thanks to a dry wind out of the southwest and the fact that not only buildings but also sidewalks were made of wood, ended up devastating some 2,000 acres, or most of the center of the city. The mayor called upon General Philip Sheridan, a Civil War hero and Chicago resident, to deal with the ensuing chaos, and the general personally patrolled the city, pistol in hand, on the lookout for the looters who, according to the local papers, were flocking into town from all over the country.

But in a few years the city was well on its way to being rebuilt, with city ordinances for construction aimed to guarantee that it would not happen again. In a few more years work was underway there to build the world's first skyscraper.

Cynics point to Mrs. O'Leary's cow as the model American urban planner. Demolition and construction, generally chaotic, have been constant in most American cities. There is nothing left in places like New York and Albany, for example, to show that they date from the 1620s. "The business of the city is business," someone once said, and often enough the only criteria for urban development has been sheer greed. But in spite of lack of planning, the social problems of rundown inner cities, chronic shortage of funds for city governments and the flight of the middle classes to the suburbs, American cities, like Chicago after the fire, have a way of bouncing back after periods of seemingly irreversible decline, stronger and more dynamic than ever.

Cities like New York and Chicago, for example, for all their very real problems, are visited by millions of tourists every year, drawn from all over the world by their fascinating ethnic diversity, wonders of modern architecture and irrepressible vitality. American cities are as diverse as the American landscape. New Orleans combines the decadent charm of a riverboat gambler with the streamlined high rises of a modern business city. Seattle and San Francisco are examples of modern cities that take advantage of the natural beauty of their settings, while Los Angeles is the city of the twenty-first century, a sprawling, decentralized, multicultural mosaic, crisscrossed by a labyrinth of freeways. ■

Seattle's Space Needle, with its slowly revolving observation deck and restaurant at the top, was built as the symbol for the city's 1962 World's Fair.

San Francisco, famous today for its cable cars, Chinatown, Fisherman's Wharf, Nob Hill mansions and Golden Gate Park, was originally called Yerba Buena when it was founded by the Spanish in 1776, and got its present name when it passed to the U.S. in 1847, during the Mexican War.

Seattle, commercial and cultural center of the Pacific Northwest, is a beautiful, dynamic city, a major port for trade with Asia and the main connection for Alaskan oil.

With its immense casinos and luxury hotels, Las Vegas, first settled by Mormons from Utah, is today an extravagant neon dreamland in the middle of the Nevada desert.

Striking advertising gimmicks, extravagant architecture, and unrestrained, innovative ideas in leisure and entertainment have made "Vegas" one of the most unusual cities in the world, a symbol of American life at its wildest extreme.

The wrought iron balconies of New Orleans' French Quarter are a reminder of the city's French and Spanish heritage. Andrew Jackson, who later became President, beat the British in a battle outside the city during the War of 1812.

"Bright lights, big city" was Jay McInerney's apt title for his popular novel about modern New York life. The waterfront, in this nocturnal view from Brooklyn Heights, dazzles the eyes and mind.

New York by night. Above, a view from the Empire State Building. The New York skyline has been a feature of innumerable films and the inspiration for musical works like Gershwin's Manhattan Rhapsody.

Chicago became known as "the windy city" not for the icy gusts off the lake in winter but for the extravagant claims made by the city's promoters when angling to make it the site for the 1893 World's Fair. They succeeded.

Seen here in a view from Hancock Tower, Chicago, a mighty giant on the shores of Lake Michigan, got its start as a French trading post in the 18th century but only began to grow into a great city in the middle of the following century.

Outdoor sculpture in downtown Chicago.
These large-scale works by Picasso, Dubuffet, Miró and Calder
are striking monuments to the city's modern, forward-looking
spirit.

The Marina City Towers, finished in 1967, and the famous Wrigley Building on Michigan Avenue (1922) represent two very different eras in the architectural history of a city in constant process of renovation.

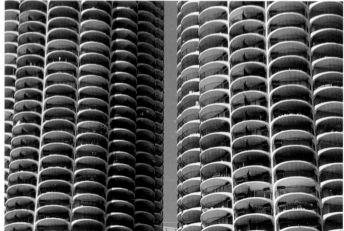

Chicago's skyscrapers are the expression, in concrete and steel, of the city's bold, adventurous, entrepreneurial spirit. Above, left, the interior of the Thompson Center; to the right the Hancock Tower.

Boston, on Massachusetts Bay, was founded by Puritans in 1630 and was the first of America's great cities and a center of the anti-British unrest which eventually led to the Revolutionary War.

In Boston, historic buildings like the Old State House (above) Quincy Market and Old North Church (below) stand unabashed next to gleaming modern giants of glass and steel.

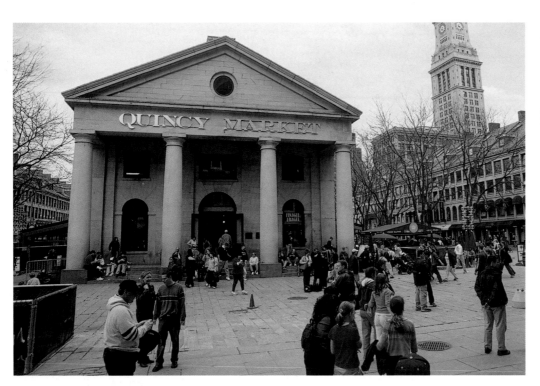

55

Landscape

The Sea

From the rocky coasts of Maine to the Florida Keys and the tropical languor of the Gulf of Mexico, from the San Juan Islands and Puget Sound to San Diego's sandy beaches, the long American seacoasts offer a seemingly endless variety of delights for the senses. Beautiful views, of course, but also that rich, ancient, ever-changing smell of the sea, the sound of the waves - from a gentle swish across the sand to the crack of breakers in a storm - and the tingle of salt spray on the skin. And don't forget the exquisite flavors of New England lobster and clam chowder, crab and salmon from the Northwest and the icy waters off Alaska, or Louisiana's famous Cajun seafood dishes.

The New England coast is cold in winter, but mild, refreshing summers and the beauties of sea and shore draw well-heeled visitors from the sweltering streets of New York, Boston and farther afield to famous resort areas like the coast of Maine, Cape Cod and Martha's Vineyard. From these same coasts Herman Melville, like many young men of his time, went to sea. Later immortalized his experiences on whaling ships in his classic *Moby Dick*, and his sojourn among Polynesian cannibals in Typee. The sea was serious business in New England then, in the 19th century, as it had been in the 18th, when maritime trade helped to make the colonists strong enough to gamble for independence from England and win.

South along the Atlantic coast the climate grows warmer. In Florida and on the Gulf of Mexico it is subtropical, and in port cities like New Orleans the air seems to have a personality of its own, dreamy, lazy and heavy with fragrances.

Southern California is known for one of the most delicious climates in the world, warm but dry, with a mild breeze off the Pacific. Going north the climate changes. Weather is similar on the coasts of northern California, Oregon and Washington, cool and often foggy in summer, with mild temperatures and wet weather in the winter.

Here great forests of enormous evergreen trees come right down to the shoreline, pebble beaches are littered with driftwood smoothed and polished by the salt sea, and gray skies mute the colors of the vegetation, creating a subtle landscape, rich in nuance, that has served as inspiration for generations of artists. ■

The Big Sur, 100 miles of ruggedly beautiful coastline, stretches from Carmel, south of Monterey, to the Hearst Castle at San Simeon. It was a little known wilderness area until in the 1960s it became popular for hiking and camping. The mountainous landscape is rich in coastal redwoods.

Mukilteo, the mainland port on the coast of Washington serving travelers to and from Whidbey Island in the Puget Sound. Many islanders commute every day to work in and around Seattle.

The Seattle-Puget Sound area is rich in wooded landscapes, pebble beaches littered with bone-white driftwood. In the distance, Mount Rainier, in the Cascades.

Hawaii's rugged, dramatic coastlines are yet another feature that make the fiftieth state the prototype of a "tropical paradise" of mild breezes and breathtaking natural beauty.

The landscape of the Hawaiian islands is one of striking variety, but never far removed from the awesome presence of the Pacific Ocean. Earliest Polynesian settlers arrived there, from across the sea, over 2000 years ago.

The volcanic islands of Hawaii are almost in the middle of the Pacific Ocean. Honolulu, the capital, is 2,397 miles from the nearest mainland port, San Francisco. The excellent climate and rich soil have nurtured flourishing populations of plant and animal life, all of which arrived, in one way or another, from across the sea.

Punaluu Beach Park, on the "Big Island", with its coconut trees and famous black sand beach, is a favorite spot for fishing snorkeling and swimming.

Florida was first visited by Spanish explorers in 1513, but the Everglades, formed by the overflow of Lake Okeechobee and covering an area of about 5,000 square miles, is still one of the wildest places in the U.S.

A pelican nonchalantly observes visitors from his home in Everglades National Park. The Everglades are rich in tropical and subtropical plant and animal life.

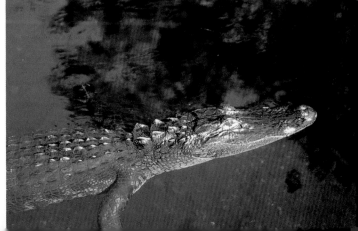

Florida's mild, subtropical climate and vegetation, and the crystalline waters that surround it are ever-present reminders that this state is the gateway to the Caribbean.

The Florida Keys, composed of limestone and coral, run 193 miles from Virginia Key, just south of Miami Beach, into the Gulf of Mexico. On the east coast of Key Largo is the largest living coral formation in North America.

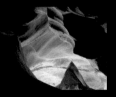

Landscape

The desert made a profound impression on Americans as they moved West, and continues to fascinate today. And no wonder. The vast expanses with mirages shimmering on the horizon, the strange, spectacular formations of rock and land, the tough yet fragile looking plant life, the sudden changes, colors full of mystery, or just the smell of the air, all make the desert an experience no one is likely to forget.

In the 19th century people coming from the humid eastern part of the country spoke of the "The Great American Desert" which they thought of as covering about a third of the nation's territory, including the arid parts of the Great Plains. Deserts in the scientific sense of the word, however, are to be found only in the Southwest.

Geographers speak of 4 great deserts, the Great Basin Desert, the Mojave, the Chihuahuan Desert, and the Sonora Desert, spread across large parts of Nevada, Utah, Arizona, California, New Mexico and Texas. Each of these contains many smaller desert areas, such as the Painted Desert, which is about 150 miles long by 15 to 50 miles wide and extends southeast from the Grand Canyon. It gets its name from the brilliantly colored rock formations of shale and sandstone, banded with vivid red, yellow, blue, white and lavender. At times the air is filled with a pink mist or purple haze of desert dust. Navaho and Hopi Indian reservations occupy a large part of the desert, and the Navahos use the colored sands for their ceremonial sand paintings.

Deserts

Death Valley, part of the Great Basin Desert, is the lowest, hottest, driest place in North America. Air temperature was recorded at 134° F. there in 1913 and ground temperature can go up to 190°. But even in the very harshest desert plant and animal life find ways to survive. Death Valley is home to the antelope squirrel and kangaroo rat, to coyotes and bobcats, and even desert bighorn sheep come down from the mountains from time to time to graze by the little waterholes. Some desert plants, like the varieties of cactus and similar plants called succulents, get by thanks to their ability to store and conserve water. The mesquite, on the other hand, uses incredibly long roots, up to 80 feet, to draw water from deep underground. Most amazing of all, perhaps, are the many varieties of desert flowers, called ephemerals, that emerge from the desert soil after the winter and spring rains, bloom for a few days or weeks and then disappear again, to wait for another chance. ■

Monument Valley, on the Navajo Indian Reservation straddling the Utah/Arizona border, is a majestic landscape of isolated red mesas, spires and sandstone buttes surrounded by sandy desert.

Desert landscapes like these, with vast skies and unearthly rock formations, have become part of the classic imagery of the American West.

Long-horned cattle still graze the arid land as they have for hundreds of years. This hardy breed's ability to live off a seemingly barren landscape and to endure the long cattle drives to Kansas City made it the favorite of ranchers in the days of the open range.

Director John Ford returned to Monument Valley again and again, using its austere, spectacular scenery as the backdrop to powerful drama in his classic westerns like *The Searchers*.

Antelope Canyon, in Arizona, is called a slot canyon. Here the Navajo sandstone was eroded to form narrow defiles often only a few feet wide.

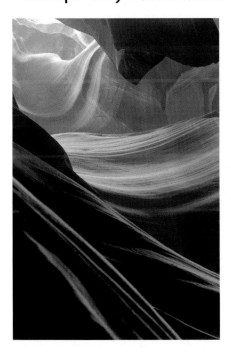

The mile-deep Grand Canyon was cut by the rushing waters of the Colorado River about 6 million years ago. Its jagged, stairstep walls have remained as they are today thanks to the semi-arid climate of the area.

Nevada is a state with vast areas of desert and strange, fascinating rock formations, like elephant rock (upper left). On the right, some varieties of the hardy desert cactus.

Landscape

The forests of the northeastern United States are home to an immense variety of trees: white and red pines, hemlock, spruce, birch, aspen, poplar, maple, oak, locust, walnut, hickory and sycamore to name only a few. Every year thousands of Americans drive up to New Hampshire, Vermont and upstate New York in the fall to see the autumn leaves turn forests into riotous mosaics of color - reds, oranges, yellows and myriad shades of brown.

The same spectacle, in less extravagant versions, can be found all the way across the northern U.S. as far as the Great Plains. Of all the trees that color the landscape at that time, the different varieties of maple, with their broad leaves, are among the most brilliant. The sugar maple is also the source of maple syrup, which is tapped in a way that is said to have been developed by the Indians. In late winter or early spring a small hole is drilled into the tree trunk at a point between two and four feet from the ground, a spout is tapped into the hole and a bucket attached. Sap flows faster or slower depending on temperature changes, and patience is an essential ingredient. When sap is boiled down it takes about 43 gallons to make one gallon of maple syrup.

Forests

In the South, magnolia, ash, and white cedar are also to be found, as well as cypress and tupelo in the swamplands. Subtropical Florida boasts palms, figs, satinwood and mangrove.

The great American forests are found in the West. Toward the end of the 19th century the United States government, alarmed by widespread cutting and clearing, established the first forest reserves. In 1905 the flamboyant president, Teddy Roosevelt, "the great outdoorsman", designated some 194 million acres as national forest and created the U.S. Forest Service to scientifically control logging and reforestation, as well as to prevent and fight forest fires.

Western forests are largely made up of coniferous trees such as the Ponderosa pine, Douglas fir, western hemlock and the giant redwood. Densest growth is to be found west of the Cascade and Coast mountain ranges in Washington, Oregon and northern California. In the rainforest of Washington's Olympic Peninsula there are trees nearly 300 feet high and eight feet in diameter.

The largest of all is the sequoia, which grows only in California. The world's largest living thing, sequoias are known to be up to 3,200 years old, with diameters of 38 feet and weighing 600 tons. ■

Colorado, with the highest mean elevation of any state in the Union, has landscape that ranges from the towering mountain peaks of the Continental Divide to gentle eastern plains.

Yosemite National Park was established in 1890 to protect and conserve the Yosemite Valley and surrounding area in the Sierra Nevada Range in central California. Here we find rock walls, domes and peaks, giant sequoia groves, deer and black bear.

Creeks tumbling into the Yosemite Valley over the edges of tributary valleys create waterfalls like the mighty Yosemite Falls, with a total drop, in three stages, of 2,425 feet.

Hawaii, the fiftieth state of the United States, is subtropical. The cooling trade winds that blow against its shores give it the mild, delicious climate that, along with its staggering natural beauty, has made the island chain a favorite vacation spot.

Views of Shenandoah National Park, as seen from Skyline Drive, which runs the full length of the park. Shenandoah is in northern Virginia, along the crest of the Blue Ridge Mountains, part of the Appalachian chain.

Landscape

Mountains

The Appalachian Mountains make up the great mountain system of the eastern United States, running about 1,500 miles from northeast Alabama to the Canadian border. These are old mountains, worn-down stumps of once much greater ranges, with areas, such as the rugged and lofty White Mountains in New England, of great beauty. The Blue Ridge Mountains on the west contain the highest elevations in this part of the country, with Mt. Mitchell in North Carolina at 6,684 feet.

In the early years of the United States the Appalachians were a barrier to western expansion and roughly corresponded to the western frontier of the original colonies. Andrew Jackson, president from 1829 to 1837, is reported to have said that the United States begins at the Alleghenies, a central Appalachian range, implying that it was only west of the mountains that people were really free of Old World influences and the true spirit of the new nation came into its own.

The Rocky Mountains are unquestionably the great American mountain range, a symbol of the country's vast, spectacular natural beauty and also its backbone, since they form the Continental Divide. Many peaks are over 13,000 feet high, and in New Mexico and on the western flanks of the Colorado ranges sharp, ragged formations and colorful rocks make for rugged, picturesque country. The Rockies are also rich in wildlife. The black bear and grizzly, the mountain lion and the wolverine are emblematic of these mountains. There are different varieties of deer, bighorn sheep and mountain goats that live up near the peaks and migrate to lower slopes for the winter, and moose that frequent northern lakes, streams and marshy areas. The bald eagle makes its home here, as do the golden eagle, the peregrine falcon and the turkey vulture as well as more common game birds like the grouse, pheasant and wild turkey.

West of the Rockies are the coastal ranges, the most important of which are the Sierra Nevada, in eastern California, and the Cascades. Mt. Whitney, in the Sierra Nevada, is the highest mountain in the United States outside Alaska, measuring 14,494 feet tall. The Cascades extend from Northern California to British Columbia. The range includes four dormant volcanoes as well as Mt. Saint Helens in southwestern Washington, long believed dormant until it erupted on May 18, 1980, causing floods and mudslides, devastating surrounding forests and covering large parts of Washington, Oregon, Idaho and Montana with volcanic ash. ■

The highway winds upward toward Berthoud Pass in Colorado, with a magnificent view of the Rocky Mountains. Rock walls, waterfalls, domes and rocky woodlands all form a part of the spectacular scenery in Yosemite National Park, on the western slopes of the Sierra Nevada.

Lush Pololu Valley on Hawaii's "Big Island" slopes gently down to the sea. The island's real name is Hawaii, and it gave its name to the entire chain.

There are five volcanoes on Hawaii's largest island, including Mauna Loa, an active volcano, 13,677 feet high. NASA observatories have been built here to take advantage of the superb visibility.

Hawaii's volcanoes erupt at irregular intervals - the most recent eruption was in 1993 - and hot lava flows are continually changing the face of the land. In time the lava solidifies into mysterious formations in a variety of colors, depending on its mineral content.

Lava from the volcanoes create mysterious, eerie landscapes like these, a vivid contrast with the lush vegetation and color of other parts of the islands. Kilauea (lower left) is the world's largest active volcano, about eight miles in circumference and 3,646 feet deep, with a lake of molten lava below its rim.

Landscape

Cities

The Sea

Deserts

Forests

Mountains

The Plains

The Plains

Much of the United States is prairie and plain, fertile soil that is also rich in mineral resources. Most of this land is to be found in the vast central area of the country, between the Appalachians and the Rocky Mountains, the Canadian border and the Rio Grande. It was here that America consolidated its strength and forged its spirit. With the Appalachians behind him the American was no longer a transplanted European looking back across the Atlantic but a new breed, busy creating a new way of life.

Settlement around the Great Lakes began almost at once after the American Revolution. First canals and later railroads facilitated links with the East and encouraged development, while natural resources laid the foundations for the region's agricultural and industrial wealth. Chicago, founded in 1830, was the second largest city in the United States only sixty years later.

Many of the settlers were immigrants, from Britain but also from Germany, the Scandinavian countries and Russia. Most of them were religious, thrifty, hardworking people, who developed a strong feeling of attachment to the land. The weather here is often harsh, with hot summers and cold winters, blizzards and tornadoes. Life was not easy, and people in rural areas created that sense of community and spirit of neighborliness and cooperation that we associate today with the traditional idea of small town America.

The Great Plains take up part of what is officially known as the Middle West and extend on to the Rocky Mountains, and it was here that the drama of the American West unfolded. Horses and cattle were introduced in the south by Spanish colonists who were in fact the first cowboys, leaving our language with words like lariat, rodeo, and corral among others. Indian tribes like the Sioux and Cheyenne, forced westward from their homes in the eastern forests, learned the art of horsemanship and, from about 1600 to the close of the 19th century, they were nomadic mounted hunters, following the vast herds of buffalo that roamed the plains.

Cattle replaced the buffalo, and by the end of the century wheat was taking the place of cattle in many areas, while ex-scout and hunter "Buffalo Bill" Cody toured the world with his Wild West show, that included Sioux Chief Sitting Bull among its attractions. Not many years later cowboys were drifting further west, to Hollywood, to ride, and sometimes star, in the first efforts of the fledgling movie industry. ∎

The green fields of the Oak Alley Plantation between New Orleans and Baton Rouge, on the Mississippi River. The great plantations, worked by slaves, were the backbone of the prosperity of the old South.

Sugarcane was the main crop on the plantation, as it was throughout much of Louisiana.

Oak trees form a 1/4 mile canopy leading to the Greek Revival style, antebellum house at Oak Alley. In contrast, above and left, old slave quarters.

The first European settlers to the area that is now the state of Virginia were Spanish Jesuits who arrived in 1570. Most of central Virginia is a rolling plateau called the Piedmont, rising into the mountain peaks and valleys of the Blue Ridge region.

Today, agriculture and mining represent a small part of the state of Virginia's economy. Livestock are beef and dairy cattle and turkeys; chief crops are tobacco, soybeans, peanuts, and corn.

People say that one of the most apparent differences between parts of the United States, from east to west, is how fast people walk. People in New York, according to this theory, walk at breakneck speed, so that if you come from some other part of the country and are out on the sidewalk you had better be ready to get out of the way or you run the risk of being run over by fast-moving, overactive New Yorkers.

In Midwestern cities people are still moving at a fairly good clip, but not nearly as fast as east-coasters. In a place like San Francisco, on the other hand, pedestrians seem to be barely moving, and the visitor from the East finds it hard to imagine how they ever manage to get anywhere at all. In Los Angeles, of course, no one walks; they either drive or jog.

But lifestyle has to do with other things besides speed, like climate, for example. Not everybody walking fast down a New York or Boston street is a stressed-out Yuppie. A lot of them are just in a hurry to get in out of the cold. And then there is mobility. Probably nothing has shaped American life so much as the automobile. The automobile made possible the growth of the suburbs; it also gave us shopping centers, drive-in restaurants, freeways and stock-car racing.

No other people in the world move as much as Americans do. Americans will move to find a better job or just to live someplace where the winters are not so awful, to "start a new life" or just because they feel like it. The "drifter" is a standard, mythical figure in movies, television and popular songs.

This mobility has no doubt had a lot to do with the United States' ongoing prosperity and ability to weather bad times and also with the traditional optimism of its people. Not so positive effects are a feeling of rootlessness and a breakdown of the sense of community that was a part of the American tradition.

Another major factor in lifestyle is leisure, a pretty recent invention. The Puritan ethic which was once supposed to inspire the nation was one of hard work. Normal people worked hard to make ends meet, and the rich were expected to work hard at getting richer. The "idle rich" no doubt existed but tended to keep quiet about it. Wealthy people in the public eye were largely self-made men who never forgot that they had

Lifestyle

come up out of poverty and never let anyone else forget it either. Having fun does not seem to be something anybody did, or at least admitted doing, until after the First World War when the "Roaring Twenties" brought in short hair and short skirts for women along with the Charleston and jazz, just as Prohibition was closing the bars and gangsters were opening speakeasies. The twenties closed with the Depression, which lasted virtually until the next war.

Life changed rapidly over this period of time. People were working fewer hours, inventions like the refrigerator and the vacuum cleaner were making housework easier and eventually eliminated the custom of keeping servants except in the homes of the very rich. By the end of the Second World War people in general had more free time and more money to spend enjoying it. Movies, the radio, and spectator sports like baseball were part of American life as early as the twenties. By the fifties, television was bringing all sorts of sports into American homes, and Hollywood was the undisputed queen of the entertainment world.

People were not just watching sports, they were also playing them. Golf went from being a rich man's game to an activity enjoyed by all sorts of people. Since the greatest part of the United States is inland, no town or city neighborhood could be without its swimming pool, and as the country got richer more and more families began to have their own pool in the backyard. The automobile also made it possible for more people to engage in outdoor activities like hunting and fishing, mountain climbing, hiking and skiing. Some time in the 1960s people began to discover the need to get fit, and city parks and suburban streets were soon filled with people jogging in bright colored shorts and specially made running shoes. A higher standard of living and another 20th century invention, the vacation, made travel a possibility not longer reserved for just the rich. Now thousands of families get out on the road every year, to go and find out what the rest of the country looks like.

Lifestyle

People

Country life

City life

Sports

Leisure

America on wheels

People

The people of the United States come from all over the world, starting with the native Americans, who are generally believed to have come from Asia, across a land bridge where the Bering Strait is now, some 26,000 years ago. These people eventually came to inhabit most of North and South America, with an immense variety of languages, tribes and social systems, from the empires of the Mayas, Aztecs and Incas to the hunters and gatherers of the Amazon jungles.

In 1513 the Spanish Hidalgo Ponce de León discovered Florida, now home to many American retirees, while supposedly searching for the Fountain of Youth. Not much later came the first English colonists, as well as the Dutch, who settled in New York and for some reason called the English Jan Kees (John Cheese), which eventually turned into Yankees. In the South the first Africans soon began to arrive, brought against their will, as slaves. People of Spanish descent were already living in Florida, the Southwest and California when these places became part of the United States. In the 19th century came the Irish, Germans, Scandinavians and Russians, Italians, Poles and Czechs. Chinese arrived to work on the building of the Union Pacific railroad to the West. Recent years have seen influxes of immigrants from the Caribbean, Central America and various parts of Asia. The people of America, at the start of a new millenium form a mosaic of colors and cultures, and thus the nation's unity is necessarily founded on a respect for diversity.

The United States is a young country, and its people have many of the qualities of the young: optimism, confidence, an eagerness to try new things and a talent for adapting to change. Balancing this headlong rush into the future is a certain need to maintain the local and ethnic traditions that link us to the past. This can be seen all over the country, in holiday celebrations, music and dance. Supermarkets, another American invention, now offer traditional foods from all over the world. One of the best examples of how openness to change combines with tradition is in the eating habits reflected in today's American cookbook, with ingredients, spices and ideas from just about every continent except Antarctica. ■

It was many years ago that someone coined the phrase, "the melting pot" to describe this country. Now, more than ever before, the people of the United States are a vast and varied mixture of races and cultures.

In the end a nation's greatest resource is its people, all their differences of race, religion, ideas and ambitions contributing to make a dynamic culture, full of vitality and hope for the future.

As happens all over the world, and probably down through history, couples find the pleasures of life twice as enjoyable when enjoyed by two.

The "body beautiful" requires some upkeep. All over the United States people from all walks of life spend time - and money - on keeping fit.

It was many years ago that
coined the phrase the melting
Now, more than ever before,
of the United States are a var
varied mixture of races and e

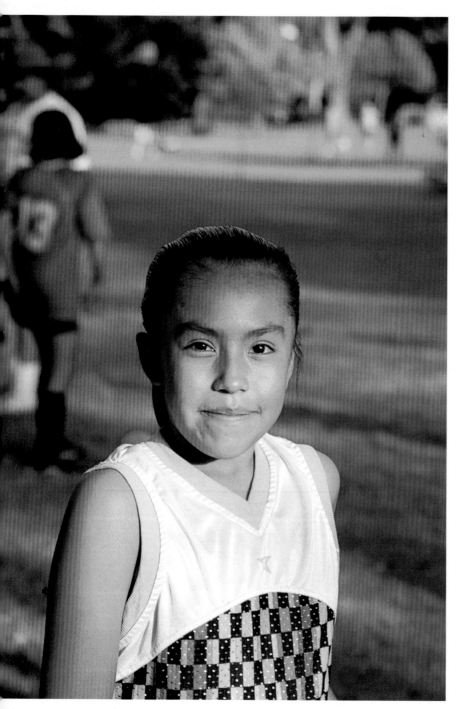

Children, wherever their parents come from, are children first and foremost.

Children from all over the country. Lower right, a little girl puts her hands on the famous sidewalk in front of Hollywood's Grauman's Chinese Theatre, where the footprints and handprints of the stars are captured forever in cement.

Smiles and frowns from another generation of young Americans, just getting started.

A Chinese wedding, a studious Jewish rabbi, the many faces of a nation.

In times before history began to be written, the first cities, the first civilizations grew up around the markets. Here, two very different faces from today's market. Old-fashioned traditions still thrive in a modern world.

An animal lover out for a winter stroll with three purebred, pint-sized chums.

Dogs and friend take a break and a contemplative look at the world around them.

Hawaii is famous for the beauty of its people as well as for its scenery. The first Hawaiians crossed the
Pacific from Polynesia in small wooden boats more than two thousand years ago.

All kinds of people, doing all kinds of jobs keep the city going, but there is always a moment in the day when its worth taking a break, to sit down, take a breath and watch the world go by around you.

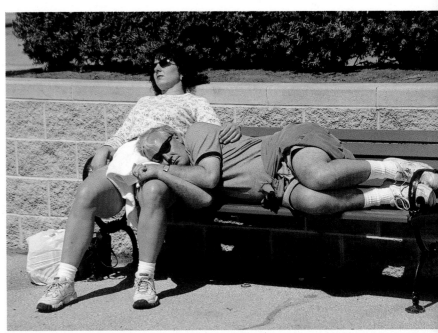

These relaxed, unhurried urbanites seem to have decided to let the rat race pass them by and take advantage of the chance to enjoy a leisurely chat, a stroll or a snooze while children have a school outing in the park.

Lifestyle

Country life

At the time of the American Revolution 95% of the population lived in rural areas and only 5% in cities. The family farm was, until the early part of the 20th century, the backbone of the society and the basis of what came to be understood as characteristic American values like self-reliance, independence, individualism and cooperation between equals. Colonists and then immigrants came to the New World with the dream of being able to own land of their own, something which was identified in the minds of people of the time with real personal freedom. In fact, for many years after the Revolutionary War ownership of land was a prerequisite to voting rights.

In the course of the 20th century the family farm gradually gave way to large scale, capital-intensive farm enterprises, so that now, though about half of the land in the United States is used for farming, 85% of agricultural production comes from these big businesses. The small farmer today not only has to be hardworking and a good enough mechanic to keep his machinery in working order, but also needs to be a tough-minded businessman capable of keeping head above water in a highly competitive field.

Mechanization has radically reduced the number of farm jobs, and the 20th century saw a gradual but massive shift of population from the country to the city. In small towns today many people once employed on farms now work in light local industries and service jobs connected with tourism. Rural areas draw visitors attracted to outdoor sports like hunting, fishing and skiing as well as camping and hiking, while families that can afford it build second homes on idyllic mountains or lake front property. The recreation industry brings income and jobs to rural areas and is an increasingly important aspect of the nation's economy.

But in many ways country life has not changed much. The pickup truck has taken the place of the horse and buggy, but the landscape, the seasons and the quirks of the weather are still there, along with the easygoing friendliness of life in the small town, where almost everyone says hello. Rodeos in the Southwest and county fairs all over rural America keep alive country traditions, while many small towns make an effort to conserve and restore their historic town centers, both to attract visitors and to keep alive a pride in their town and its history. ■

Livestock raising, particularly of beef and dairy cattle, has played an important role in American agriculture since the very beginning of our history. The simple, dignified structure of the American barn has long been a familiar part of the rural landscape, while modern windmills like those below still seem like something out of science fiction.

The tractor and the pickup truck are today's farmers basic tools, like the plow and the horse and buggy of years gone by.

Harpers Ferry, West Virginia. Here the Potomac and Shenandoah rivers meet, forming the borders of Maryland, Virginia and West Virginia. Abolitionist John Brown's raid on the Harpers Ferry arsenal in 1859 was one of the events that led to the Civil War.

Even on the Hawaiian islands we find meadows and plains much like those of the central United States, offering good grazing land for livestock.

The Indians of the American Southwest are famous for their weaving. Colorful blankets and tapestries are handcrafted using time-honored traditional methods, patterns and motifs. Weaving is done with thread made from the wool of sheep raised by the Indians themselves.

Drums and intricately decorated pottery also form a part of the craft tradition of various Indian tribes living in the mostly arid regions of the Arizona, New Mexico and Colorado.

Lifestyle

People

Country life

City life

Sports

Leisure

America on wheels

City life

For years the city was a place mothers warned about. Those bright lights and pretty women will dazzle your eyes, they would say, and smooth-talking city slickers will play you for a fool. It never seemed to do much good. "There's one born every minute," the showman P. T. Barnum once said, referring to suckers, and many were the country boys that woke up after their first night in the city with an aching head and empty pockets.

Times have changed of course. Country boys are not so easy to fool nowadays, and there are not nearly as many of them either. Every city worthy of the name, however, still has a number of places available where the out-of-towner in search of a good time can be quickly and painlessly separated from his money. The city still means excitement, and city lights continue to draw young people, not just with the promise of better paid jobs and career advancement, but also with all they have to offer in terms of entertainment, culture, education, sports and opportunities for meeting people.

City life has its disadvantages, but for the convinced urbanite whatever inconveniences the city might occasion are more than compensated for by the possibilities of experiencing the buzz, verve and excitement of crowded streets and the tinselly glamour of city lights. Improvements in public transport have meant fewer people going to work in their cars, and a lowering in traffic density means less pollution and noise, making the city a more comfortable place to live.

The basic unit of the city is the neighborhood, and many old neighborhoods have a character that is distinctly their own. Italian, Greek, Polish or German neighborhoods, and of course the famous Chinatowns, offer restaurants and specialty food stores, and many celebrate neighborhood festivals at some time during the year. Most American cities have at least one university, which often gives the neighborhood around it its own particular, somewhat bohemian style, with a variety of cafés, bars, restaurants and bookshops, catering to a young clientele. The American city today is far more sophisticated than anyone would ever have imagined a hundred - or even fifty - years ago, and on the streets of almost any city you can find an exciting, cosmopolitan mixture of people from all over the world. ■

Snow and freezing weather in winter are no strangers to many of America's great cities. City dwellers shrug, grin and bear it.

Bustling city streets are the nervous, vibrant pulses of urban life, people living and working in the modern, city environment of concrete, steel and glass.

The city dweller finds space to breathe, to stroll or cycle through the many parks and along riversides and lakefronts, while intrepid cyclists venture undaunted out into the city traffic.

A snowfall in Central Park, New York, (left) is a beautiful sight, but doesn't make life any easier for drivers. Downtown traffic is tough, and most residents use the efficient networks of public transport when they can.

Some city dwellers opt for the bicycle, a clean, quick way of getting around for people with strong legs who enjoy the wind in their faces. The San Francisco cable car, on the right, is a favorite with visitors to the city.

City residents can find fresh produce, meat and fish at public markets like Seattle's famous old Pike Place Market or the market at New York's Grand Central Station.

Establishments like Boston's Quincy Market (above) or this wholesale/retail fish market in Chicago (below) offer seemingly endless possibilities for the gourmet cook and amateur alike, as well as a feast for the eye.

Greenwich Village, a favorite of New York bohemians, artists, writers and theater people since the '20s, is full of bars and cafes, like this one, decorated in a striking, high-tech style.

Tourists and local residents alike enjoy the Seattle sun outside the many cafes and restaurants.

Cafés, restaurants and dining halls where people enjoy a snack, a meal or the pleasure of one another's company, while the city's department stores offer everything from basic necessities to luxuries that are hard to resist.

Music of all sorts and in all sorts of places is an essential part of city life, especially in fine weather. Above right, a pint-sized urban music lover enjoys a snack.

Lifestyle

Sports

Sports

Sports play an important role in American life in a variety of ways. Playing sports in school is a crucial part of the growing up experience for countless young people, and even the seasons of the year have their sports connotations - fall means football, winter is basketball, spring track and summer, of course, is baseball. Sports are entertainment, keeping millions glued to their TV sets all day Sunday and several other nights of the week. They also make legends. Sports like boxing have given us those classic true-life stories of young men from underprivileged backgrounds who made good. Men like Joe Louis, Rocky Marciano or the world famous Muhammad Ali, who with no more advantages than their own skill and courage fought their way to fame and fortune.

The three major national sports are all American inventions. Football, initially much like European soccer, was being played in the eastern U.S. in the 1820s. Professional football, played by ex-college players, started around the turn of the century, and the NFL came into existence in 1921. Franchises, which today are worth millions, then cost $100 each.

Basketball was invented by a Dr. James Naismith at the YMCA training school in Springfield, Massachusetts, in 1891, and as early as early as 1898 the first professional league was formed. The introduction of the jump shot in the 1930s speeded up the game, but it was not until the 1970s, with an expanded NBA, that basketball became the crowd-drawing equivalent of professional leagues in other sports. Basketball is played in more countries than any other team ball game, and players like Michael Jordan are international celebrities, familiar all over the world.

Traditionally, the "national pastime" is baseball. Union troops played baseball during the Civil War, and the National League was founded as long ago as 1876, the American League in 1900. Players like Ty Cobb, "Dizzy" Dean, "Babe" Ruth and Joe DiMaggio were national heroes in their day, and Hollywood cashed in on their fame to make movies about their lives.

Americans today play and follow a wide variety of sports. Tennis has been popular for years, ice hockey is a favorite in the Northeast and different types of car races take place all over the country. Horse racing, of course, is the "sport of kings". Golf, once restricted to the wealthier strata of society, is today the favorite sport of millions, with the advantage that it can be played by people of all ages. ■

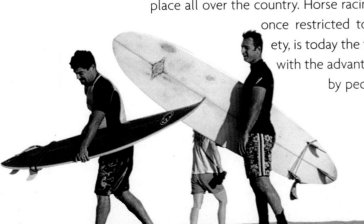
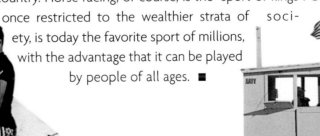

Ice hockey is a fast-moving, electrifying sport, particularly popular in the Northeastern United States. This game is on the rinks at the north end of New York's Central Park.

The stark winter landscape of Central Park, New York City, in the snow is the backdrop for this amateur rugby match, with players so involved in their game they forget

Originating in England in the early 19th century, rugby is a fast moving sport similar to soccer and football. As in football, the problem is to get the ball across the goal line. There is tackling, but no blocking.

Though overshadowed by crowd pleasers like football and basketball, track has always been an important sport at high schools and on college campuses across the country. Here, the two Harvard teams up a sweat.

Sports appeal to people of all ages, including schoolchildren like these girls at soccer practice in a park in sunny Albuquerque, New Mexico.

Golf was invented in Scotland, and the earliest written record of the game is in the Scottish Acts of Parliament from - amazingly - 1457. It was almost five centuries later when golf caught on in America, but since then it has certainly made up for lost time.

Baseball is also a traditional college sport. Uniforms at Harvard University seem to have changed very little since the early 1900s.

Baseball is the great American summer sport. Here, the Sacramento River Cats, a minor league club, playing at home in Sacramento, California, with the stands full of spectators.

One of the great outdoor sports, baseball is played by school and amateur teams, major and minor league professionals all over the country. And wherever it is played it is sure to draw a crowd.

The ocean, the pound of the waves and rich sea smell, draws all kinds of sports enthusiasts for a variety of activities. Surfing has been the rage on the Southern California coast since the sixties, while windsurfing is a somewhat newer development.

The leisurely flowing Charles River in Cambridge, Massachusetts, is the usual spot for practice for the Harvard University crew and kayak teams.

Lifestyle

Leisure

Leisure means time, time to enjoy life. In the 20th century the 40-hour week and the economic prosperity that was consolidated after World War II meant that ordinary people had free time and money to spend on it, and leisure was no longer a privilege reserved for the rich. It took a while for the world to realize just what that was going to mean. The people who invented the movie camera did not expect it to amount to much more than another sideshow attraction, but a few years later Charlie Chaplin was the most famous person in the world. Entertainment was big business, and Hollywood was the entertainment capital of the world.

Then came television, wich scared the life out of Hollywood moguls for a while, until they realized there was room for everybody. At the same time, in the 50s, young people were listening to the radio and going down to the local record shop to buy songs by people like Bill Haley and the Comets, Chuck Berry, Little Richard, Jerry Lee Lewis, and, of course, Elvis. It was an explosion. They called it Rock 'n Roll. Parents hated it, but kids loved it. And the kids won.

Leisure is more than just entertainment of course. For many it means the chance to do things: sports, like golf, or hobbies, from model railroading to collecting fruit crate labels or raising violets. The 50s, which marked the formation of our modern lifestyle in so many ways, also saw the beginning of the do-it-yourself craze, and thousands of Americans became amateur electricians or carpenters in their off hours. Life in the suburbs made it possible for people to get their hands in the dirt, reconnecting perhaps with an old agricultural heritage still in their genes, and for many people gardening is a favorite free-time activity. Others prefer to spend their free time keeping fit, jogging or mountain-biking, for example, working out in a gym, taking dance classes or learning karate or Tai-chi. Leisure also means time to enjoy your friends, and make new ones, at neigh-borhood parties, in clubs and social organizations. Vacation time is a chance to travel, to get out and see the country, and can be anything from a visit to Disneyland to a canoeing trip down the Grand Canyon.

Leisure, in the end, is also the sublime privilege of not doing anything at all. Sitting out on the porch on a summer evening, for example, just watching the sun go down. ■

Oceans, lakes and rivers, just about any body of water has something about it that soothes, relaxes. And a day on the water leaves you wonderfully refreshed.

There is no better way to get close to nature than walking, taking the time to appreciate the details, look around you, feel the silence, smell the air.

Skating combines outdoor, athletic activity with an esthetic of rhythm and grace. Dancing on wheels. A pleasure for all ages.

Parks and lakefronts provide pleasant settings for getting exercise, whether you are just taking a stroll or getting in shape for your next marathon.

Leisure can be a time to get in touch with nature, give your artistic side a chance to come out or, when the weather's right, to enjoy a picnic lunch with friends.

Fishing, skating, cycling or just taking a walk are only some of the ways to enjoy Chicago's magnificent lakefront on lake Michigan, with the city's towering skyscrapers in the background.

The twilight years mean time to enjoy old friends and make new ones. Or to find a harmony of body and spirit by studying an ancient oriental discipline like Tai Chi.

Winter in the city has its own special magic, the silent glide of skaters across the ice or a raucous snowball fight. On cold winter days hundreds of Americans go out to a park to skate on a natural pond.

A lone cross-country skier makes his way through a scene of stark winter beauty in New York's Central Park.

The Rockefeller Plaza skating rink is smack in the center of Manhattan, between 5th and 6th Avenue, attracting tourists and residents alike.

The Metropolitan Museum of Art, popularly known as "The Met" (left and below) is the United States' largest and most comprehensive art museum, with collections that range from art, pottery and sculpture of ancient civilizations to modern art, photography and design. Above, the Natural History Museum.

302

Jazz, a uniquely American form of music, began with street bands like this one that played at weddings and funerals and in cafés in the Storyville district of New Orleans.

Blues, jazz, Dixieland, ragtime, all grew out of the musical tradition of work songs, laments and spirituals of African American slaves in the Old South.

Las Vegas is a city of light, open 24 hours a day. "The Strip" with its casinos, nightclubs and luxury hotels, is famous for its gaudy, ingenious neon signs.

Legendary entertainers are an important part of the attraction of Las Vegas, which is one of the fastest growing cities in the U.S.

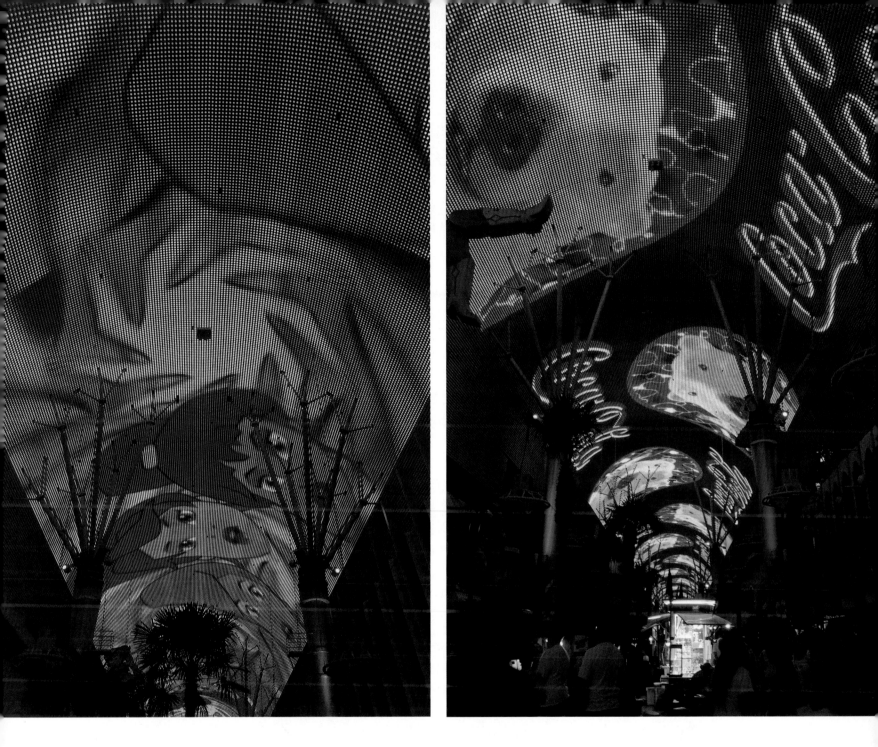

This street on "The Strip" in Las Vegas is covered with a screen that is alive with moving images, yet another symbol of the city's ongoing, high tech innovation.

New Orleans' "Mardi Gras", with its costumes, parades and music and the whole city in the streets, is one of the world's best known carnival celebrations.

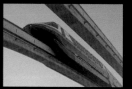

Lifestyle

People

Country life

City life

Sports

Leisure

America on wheels

America on wheels

In 1898 railroad lines ran from coast to coast, and there were already 50 automobile manufacturing companies in the United States. But while the railroad had clearly played an important part in turning the country into an industrial and economic power, most people at the turn of the century saw the "horseless carriage" as a noisy plaything for the rich, belching smoke, frightening horses and moving at breakneck speeds of up to twenty-five miles an hour. Ten years later a 45-year-old engineer with a grade-school education named Henry Ford brought out the first Model T and announced that he was going to make cars "for the great multitude". Ford's revolutionary assembly line production system made it possible to sell cars at prices ordinary people could afford, and in 20 years he sold over 15 million Model T's in the United States alone, changing the face of the nation forever.

The automobile found a perfect match in the restless, individualistic American spirit. For the Model T, Ford said customers could have "any color they want, as long as it's black", but by the end of World War II car manufacturers and the advertising agencies that were working for them understood that the car, like a lot of other consumer goods, was also an expression of the owner's personality. Hot-rodders were customizing the bodies of their cars, as well as souping up the engines, and car manufacturers strove to beat the competition by coming up with design changes for each year's new model. Car design also reflected the mood of the nation. Towards the end of the 1950s, for instance, in a period of unprecedented prosperity and national self-confidence, cars got longer and wider every year, with more chrome and bigger tailfins. By 1959 cars had got as big as they reasonably could, and the success of imported foreign cars, particularly the Volkswagen "Beetle", led American car-makers to come out with their own "compacts".

The image of the "open road" has been a part of American folk consciousness from the poet Walt Whitman to Jack Kerouac's classic Beat Generation novel, "On the Road", the 60s movie, "Easy Rider" and uncountable rock 'n roll songs. For many people the key to the adventure of the road is the motorcycle, and the king of motorcycles is the mythic Harley-Davidson. While motorcycles all over the world are generally built for speed, agility and handling on rough terrain, the Harley-Davidson, fondly known as "the Hog", is essentially a "road bike", a big, heavy, comfortable vehicle built for the adventure of the endless highway. ∎

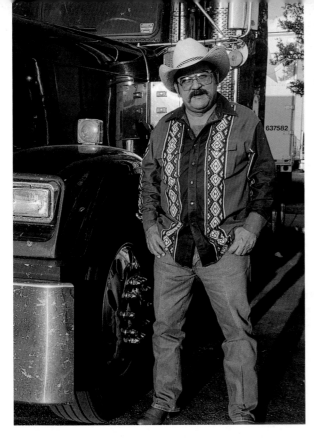

The semi is a symbol of American life on the road. These great, gleaming, powerful vehicles move merchandise along highways and freeways all over the United States.

The taxi, whisking shoppers, tourists and business people to myriad destinations, is a vital part of city life.

Once reserved for movie stars, big-time crooks, visiting statesmen and oil billionaires, the limousine, now in its stretch version, is often used to carry travelers from airport to hotel and vice versa.

The used car market has something for everybody - and for just about every pocket book - from the limousine to a classic Karmann-Ghia, to a Corvette that used to belong to an old lady who never used it except to drive to church on Sunday.

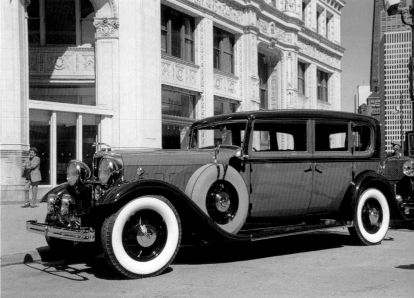

Some things don't change, like the classic old gas station pump above. Others, like these two classic cars from very different eras, need a lot of elbow grease to keep them in shape.

Big, brash and with a beauty all its own, the Harley Davidson, like Coca-Cola, is a symbol of the American lifestyle that is known all over the world. Once a symbol of youth and rebellion, Harley owners nowadays come from every walk of life.

Yellow school buses like this one - the model has changed only slightly down through history - have been taking American children to school all over the country for well over fifty years.

Legendary Grand Central station, in New York City was built when the railroad was king TA, is still a bustling center for commuters and that select minority who prefer the old-fashioned comfort of the train for long distance travel.

The original route of Chicago's "L" - short for elevated train - gave the city's downtown area its name, "The Loop". The "L" still circles the Loop, then branches off to the north, west and south of the city, and is only one part of the Chicago Transit Authority system, one of the most modern and efficient public transport networks in the world.

The New York subway system plays a key role in making the great city work. The first subway system in the city went into operation in 1904, and at one time there were four independent subway companies, which were eventually unified.

The complex subway network is a kind of microcosm, a world within a world, and reflects the same mixture of diverse cultures and races as the streets overhead.

The American highway, the open road, is the backbone of the nation's economy and at the same time a symbol of the American dream, opening to all the endless wonders of a vast and beautiful country.

A nation's architecture is a reflection of both the spirit of its people and the land in which they live. In architecture, as in so many other aspects of American life, the vast expanse of the country played an important role. One of the major characteristics of American architecture - and one which never fails to strike the visiting foreigner - is the prodigal use of land. The American's idea of a house is a heritage of the colonial past, when land was cleared and houses erected to stand alone in the midst of the landscape. Thus the typical American house is invariably conceived of as surrounded by space on all four sides, and this is stubbornly maintained, even when that space is little more than symbolic and only two or three feet separate one house from its neighbor. The one-story or split-level, ranch style homes that came into vogue in the fifties sprawled across the landscape as if boasting that owners had more land than they knew what to do with. Even skyscrapers have almost always been built as individual, free-standing towers, piercing the sky like the church spires of a secular religion.

Wood has been the primary construction material since the earliest colonies of the 17th century when the continent, from the Atlantic coast to the Mississippi, was still covered by the world's largest temperate forest. Houses were built with the felled timbers of this forest: oaks, pines, hemlocks and chestnuts, dense woods, impervious to insects and rot. The 19th century, and particularly the Industrial Revolution, brought new building processes and materials, but the lessons of wood lingered on with American builders, who have tended to look at their work with a carpenter's eye, in terms of arrangements of folded planes and two-dimensional objects. Thus the tradition of American architecture is sharply distinguished from countries such as Italy, France and Spain where it was historically conceived in masonry. The novelist Charles Dickens, struck by this difference while travelling in the United States, wrote of "sharp outlines," "razor-like edges" and the "clean cardboard colonnades" of New England.

During much of its history American architecture was, inevitably, based on European ideas, but these ideas were filtered through particular American conditions and sensibility. In the late 18th and early 19th centuries much of the inspiration came from Italy, but the architects attempting to emulate the monumental stone

Architecture

architecture of the Italian Renaissance knew their models through pattern books and not first hand, and the results are more suggestive of American rationalism and idealism than of Mediterranean sensuality. The Neo-classical style of buildings like the White House and the Capitol make a symbolic link between the new nation and the classical tradition of Greek democracy, but are, in the end, uniquely American.

Civic architecture remained stuck in a classical rut during the 19th and much of the 20th century, and America's most striking buildings were confident, often extravagant symbols of a commercial society - urban banks, company offices and department stores like the Marshall Field building in Chicago. The Victorian period saw the introduction of a variety of styles, the most significant of which was the Gothic Revival, taking its inspiration from French and English models from the 12th to the 15th centuries, and great private homes were often specially designed in this elaborate style to express the flamboyant personalities of their owners.

The high point of this commercial influence and America's most characteristic contribution to architecture, the skyscraper, was not the result of an aesthetic movement but rather of a combination of technological and economic circumstances, including the development of structural steel and the elevator, the high price of urban property and zoning restrictions like New York's famous setback laws of 1916.

American architecture has long been open to experiment, particularly along utilitarian lines, resulting at times in brilliantly designed but totally unlivable buildings but also providing American houses with the best heating, insulation and plumbing in the world as early as the middle of the 19th century. In the 20th century American architecture came into its own and, though influenced by the ideas of European Modernism, developed along varied, often eclectic lines. One of the foremost figures, revolutionizing design for the home, was Frank Lloyd Wright, who combined Modernism's use of cheap, mass-produced materials and the concept of the house as machine with individuality of expression and a profound sensitivity for the building's natural setting.

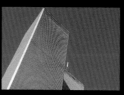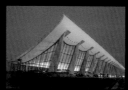

Architecture

Public Buildings

Traditional homes

Contemporary homes

Public Buildings

If we consider that public architecture is an expression of the collective spirit, it is not surprising that the earliest examples of interest are to be found in the colonial churches of 17th and 18th century New England. With their sharp, uncluttered lines, these churches, generally simple rectangular structures with angular adjoining towers, perfectly embody the sober, Puritan spirituality that was the bedrock of that society. Government buildings during that same period, in the English Georgian style throughout most of the 18th century, were, on the other hand, massive, heavy structures built to express the authority of the institutions they represented.

The period after the American War of Independence soon saw the beginnings of the Neo-classical style with columns, domes and rotundas that recalled the birthplace of democracy in ancient Greece. The University of Virginia, designed in this style by former president Thomas Jefferson and finished in 1825, often called America's finest man-made object, is a meeting of architectural idealism and a profound sense of landscape, qualities which recur much later in the work of Frank Lloyd Wright.

During the 19th century, particularly after the Civil War, public buildings, emblematic of the nation's growing strength and confidence, grew larger and increasingly elaborate. The railroads, at once the motors of progress and the dominant economic forces of the day, built practical monuments to their power like the Union Station in Chicago, Grand Central Station in New York and Boston's North Station. Toward the end of the century architecture was going vertical, in a trend that began with the ten-story Montauk Building, built in Chicago in 1882 and the first to be called a skyscraper, and reached its peak in the 1920s with great Chicago and New York skyscrapers like the Tribune Tower (1925), the Chrysler Building (1930) and the Empire State Building (1931 - 1,250 feet tall).

Taller buildings have gone up since, but in subsequent years architecture in America became far more eclectic and imaginative, as well as finding it necessary to search for new ways to meet the technical challenges of a rapidly changing world, as the airport supplanted the railroad station and the shopping center took the place of the great urban department store. Following the Great Depression commercial architecture with its brash monuments to corporate power ceased to dominate the scene, and new works like the Guggenheim Museum in New York and Yale University's Beinecke Library signaled a turn towards today's more complex and sophisticated cultural environment. ■

The Manhattan skyline, dominated by the some of the world's tallest buildings, is an imposing and thought-provoking symbol of civilization in the 20th century.

Boston is one of the oldest cities in America. Here venerable buildings like the old Trinity Church (left), built in 1872 - 1877 in the Romanesque style of architect H. H. Richardson, now sit at the feet of modern giants.

Skyscrapers

The exterior fire escapes on the facades are a trademark of New York's SoHo district, whose name is an acronym for "south of Houston Street". Once a warehouse district, artists began moving in during the '60s, using upper floors as studio lofts while ground floor display areas turned into art galleries and cafes.

Neo-gothic skyscrapers from the 20s stand side by side with the sleek forms of buildings from the end of the century.

The Twin Towers, 110 floors high, with their stream lined, ultra-modern design and imposing height, are among the more recent symbols of New York's seemingly limitless upward expansion.

Though often built within the same urban area, each skyscraper stands on its own, making its own particular architectural statement.

Different periods have had very different ideas about decorative and architectural beauty. All over the city we can find sharp contrasts between the new and the old.

Contrasting approaches to the problem of the window. Thanks to structural pillars, skyscraper walls do not support the weight of the building and can thus be made entirely of glass, taking maximum advantage of available natural light.

Airports

Airports, like this one in Denver, Colorado, meet the design problems involved in a complex which must include passenger terminals, hangars and cargo terminals, as well as shops and restaurants

Small airports like the one shown below form a vast network that makes it possible to travel by air to all parts of the country.

Public buildings like the planetarium of the New York Museum of Natural History and the museum in San Francisco designed by Mario Botta, are often startling for the boldness of their design.

The Guggenheim Foundation

has built museums all over the world but the most famous is the New York Guggenheim designed by Frank Lloyd Wright and considered one of the architect's most significant buildings. It was opened after his death, in 1959.

New York's Metropolitan Museum of Art, built in 1895, shows the classical Greek columns and massive, monumental style typical of many 19th century public buildings.

The vast entrance hall to the Metropolitan, like the entrance to a Greek temple, seems built expressly to impose a sense of respect on visitors. In the interior, more modern concepts make good use of natural light.

This church in San Francisco, with the powerful, upward thrust of its ceiling, is an example of modern trends in church architecture.

Churches

In St. Ignatius Chapel in Seattle the architect Steven Holl creates an atmosphere of spirituality through the use of an austere simplicity of line reminiscent of the medieval monasteries.

Five years of planning and four years of construction went into the building of the U.S. Force Academy Chapel, that was designed by the architectural firm Skidmore, Owings and Merrill.

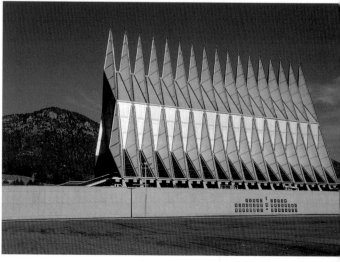

Saint Miguel de Asís Church in Taos is the oldest church in New Mexico, a model of the imposing, massive simplicity of style characteristic of the old Spanish architecture of the Southwest.

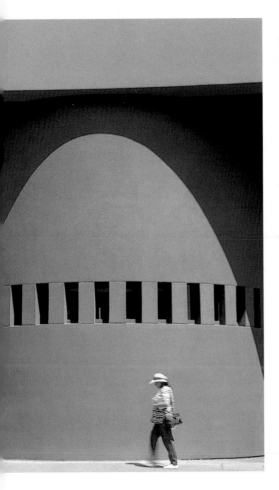

Radically modern design and an innovative treatment of light define this library designed by Ricardo Legorreta, in San Antonio, Texas.

Libraries

The capitol building in Austin, Texas, in the Neo-classical style commonly associated with the dignity of government buildings

Government buildings

The imposing facade of the New York Stock Exchange building on Wall Street is another example of the use of architectural elements from ancient Greek temples to create an impression of majesty and power.

The Statue of Liberty, the Arch of Triumph in Washington Square in New York and the Monument to the Confederate Dead in Austin, Texas, are some examples of public monuments.

Monuments & Memorials

Public statues are built to honor historical personages or, like the Indian statue in Albuquerque, New Mexico, on the left, to recall some moment of our history.

Bridges, which often employed new materials and construction techniques, stand today as monuments to daring feats of engineering and to the courage of the men who built them.

Shops

Like Spavionavigli on the previous pages, 20th Century is a smart New York furniture shop catering to a sophisticated clientele. This shop features copies of furniture from the '40s and '50s.

Store windows make downtown city streets an ongoing, ever-changing show, with everything from the world of fashion to visual lessons in science.

Architecture for commerce requires its own particular way of dealing with space. Consumers expect to be dazzled, entertained and surprised. Shopping is, after all, one of America's most popular pastimes.

Universities

Harvard University, with its main campus on the Charles River in Cambridge, Massachusetts, a few miles west of downtown Boston, is the oldest university in the United States. It was founded in 1636, originally to educate Puritan ministers.

The sober elegance of the buildings that enclose Harvard Yard are a living memory of colonial times in one of our most prestigious universities. Alumni include a long list of great American philosophers, writers and statesman, among them President John F. Kennedy.

After his two terms as president, Thomas Jefferson founded the University of Virginia in Charlottesville, Virginia, near his home at Monticello. Jefferson chose the site, planned the campus and designed the famous rotunda at its center.

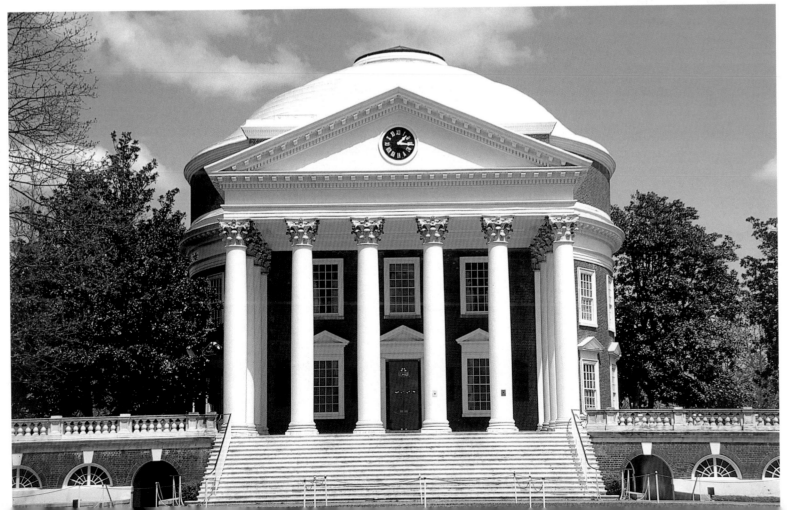

Jefferson used the Pantheon of Rome as his model for the rotunda. The masterpiece of the American neoclassical style, in 1976 the American Institute of Architects voted it "the proudest achievement of American architecture in the past 200 years".

The W hotel at Union Square in Manhattan is the fruit of an extensive conversion of the landmark Guardian Life building, a magnificent granite and limestone structure built in 1911 in a traditional European architectural style.

The 20-story former office building is now a 270-room hotel with 15 deluxe suites. It features a warm, luminous living room, gardens and comfortable lounge areas.

The hotel offers an ambience of contemporary luxury, clean lines, luminous spaces and an exquisite attention to detail.

The Dylan Hotel occupies the former Chemist's Club building in downtown Manhattan, between Madison and Park Avenue.

The Hudson Hotel in New York City, is a melting pot of styles and ideas, a reflection and distillation of New York itself. Behind its layers of contrasting styles and environments is the intention of making the hotel an urban adventure in itself.

The Hudson represents a democratization of style, in the spirit of the times we live in, young at heart, with the emphasis on unique personal experience, emotion and individuality rather than status or money.

The interiors of the Hacienda del Sol Hotel in Tucson, Arizona maintain the traditional style of old Spain, with delicately designed tiles on the walls, solid, comfortable furniture and a stylish use of light and local plants.

The Hacienda del Sol Hotel is an example of traditional Spanish American architecture in a modern context. Arched porches, ceramic pots, leaded windows and the protruding ends of rounded, wooden beams are all elements of classic Spanish architecture, which were carried on in the American southwest.

Architecture

Public Buildings

Traditional Homes

Contemporary Homes

Traditional Homes

The first American original, the New England saltbox, developed in the 17th century, was a simple, two-story house with the roof extended in the rear to cover a pair of additional first floor rooms, and it made for a snug, cozy structure that kept the family warm through the hard New England winter. In much of the United States, however, there are hot summers as well as cold winters, and a design was needed that would provide year round comfort. The solution was a house that was compact at the core but opened up to nature in fine weather with an attached wooden porch. Traditional American homes, whether Colonial, Georgian, Federalist, Greek Revival, Neo-Gothic, Italianate, Queen Anne, or whatever, are generally two-sometimes three-story structures, usually of wood but sometimes made of brick, with a porch, sloping roof and often dormers on the third floor. Homes that were variations on these classic styles continued to be built well into the 20th century. The American architect, more a practical man of business than an intellectual, saw architectural history as a sort of Sears Catalogue of possibilities to be adapted to the customer's tastes, needs and pocketbook.

The last distinct type of traditional home was the American Foursquare, which was designed to provide a family of relatively modest means with a dignified looking house. The structure was a cube, with 4 square rooms above, 3 rooms and an entrance hall on the first floor and a porch at the front that ran the full width of the house. Built from the late 1800s until well into the 1930s, houses like this are still to be found all over the country and have their place in the imagination as the typical American family home.

The broad front porch, running through American architecture from colonial times, was born as an adaptation to climactic conditions, but had a social significance as well. The English home is immanently private while southern Europe is the culture of the marketplace, but the porch, uniquely American in this way, is a transitional zone that is both public and private, where people sit out in front of their homes, casually conversing with neighbors passing by on the sidewalk. The world of the American Foursquare, like the small-town world of the movies of Frank Capra, was one of easy-going, familiar social exchange. A world which, along with the pedestrian, has to a great extent disappeared thanks to the combined effects of television and the automobile.

In 1770 Thomas Jefferson, at the age of 27, recently admitted to the bar, began work on Monticello, a neoclassical mansion on the top of a small hill on his 640-acre estate in Virginia. Jefferson lived at Monticello for 56 years. In 1926 it was declared a national shrine.

In San Francisco, many beautiful, ornate old Victorian style homes like these have been turned into apartments.

This proud mansion on the famous Oak Alley Plantation in Louisiana is a superbly preserved example of the Greek Revival style, built in 1839. 28 classic columns surround the house, matching in number the 28 ancient live oak trees, believed to have been planted in 1718, that form the "Oak Alley" leading up to the house.

Examples of the Greek Revival style which was overwhelmingly popular, particularly in the South, after the American Revolution. Typical of these buildings are the use of classic columns and the porches which extend at least across the front of the house and sometimes go all the way around it.

These great mansions, almost always white, were symbols of their owners' wealth and power but were also built with an eye to keeping their residents cool and comfortable through the hot southern summers.

The porch is also an important element in these urban homes, probably built in the second half of the 19th century. Lines and angles seem much sharper and more severe than the smooth, flowing lines of the southern mansion.

Architect William Hoffman designed his home in Taos, New Mexico, based on the model of the traditional adobe home of the Spanish southwest, houses adapted to the particular climatic conditions of the region.

Lamps and decorative pieces in the Hoffman home - the finishing touches - create an environment of simple, understated beauty. Constant references to the past, but with a modern, personal twist.

This luxurious Miami home blends with the lush Florida environment while using concepts like the traditional Spanish balcony that lead us back to the colonial history of this state, so close to the Caribbean.

Typical of the familiar Main Street in small town America are structures like these, simple frame houses with no pretensions, built to last.

The single-story bungalow, an idea that originally came from India, first became popular in California in the mid-twentieth century. The wooden porch, as seen below, has been a characteristic feature of the American home for centuries.

Architecture

Public Buildings

Traditional Homes

Contemporary Homes

Contemporary Homes

The contemporary home is the result of the interaction of a variety of ideas and possibilities, in continual evolution. Just as the skyscraper would not have been possible without the development of steel and reinforced concrete, the modern home would not look like it does today were it not for the technology and materials created and successively modified in the course of the 20th century.

Along with technical innovations, radical changes were taking place during the early part of the century that also changed the way that people looked at building a home. Movements like Cubism in modern art had an important effect on architecture, leading to the acceptance, among architects, if not always among the general public, of radical simplicity as an esthetic value in itself. New tendencies in design, particularly the influential Bauhaus School in Germany, adamantly rejected the frills and superfluous decoration of the Victorian home and took utilitarianism as their battle cry, a concept that was also fundamental for modern architects.

Social changes also played their part. Servants became a thing of the past except for the very, very rich. Families became smaller as couples chose, for a variety of reasons, to have fewer children. Feminism and changes in women's role in society not only created a demand for more convenient and easy-to-clean appliances, surface materials and kitchen design but also brought a tendency to bring down walls and make the cooking area another part of the common living space, often separated only by a convenient, multi-use counter. Finally, the growth of the suburbs and the increase in the number of families with a second home have made it possible for more and more people to choose and even to take an active part in designing their "dream house".

Today, architecture for the home is eclectic, open to a seemingly inexhaustible range of possibilities and apparently unconstrained by prejudice or tradition. Nonetheless, certain characteristics consistently appear. One is the use of large expanses of glass to bring an abundance of natural light into the home, while at the same time opening up the home to its environment, blurring the barriers between outside and inside. Modern residential architecture reflects our time's commitment to a respect for the environment, and modern homes are conceived, designed and built to fit harmoniously into their natural setting as well as to take the fullest possible advantage of all its aesthetic value. ■

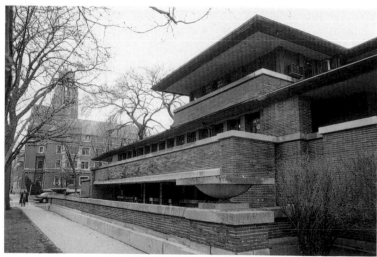

Not one to mince words, Frank Lloyd Wright flatly claimed to have founded modern architecture, and there is no question that he was one of the key figures in its beginnings. Wright arrived in Chicago in 1887, while the city was in a frenzy of reconstruction after the great fire. The homes he built in the Chicago suburb of Oak Park in the Prairie Style mark the transition to what was to become the contemporary home.

These homes, built by Frank Lloyd Wright before the turn of the century, seem almost traditional to us now but represented, in their day, the beginnings of radical change. Wright was a pioneer in the use of open spaces without partitions in the home, in the use of new technologies and in his profound respect for nature.

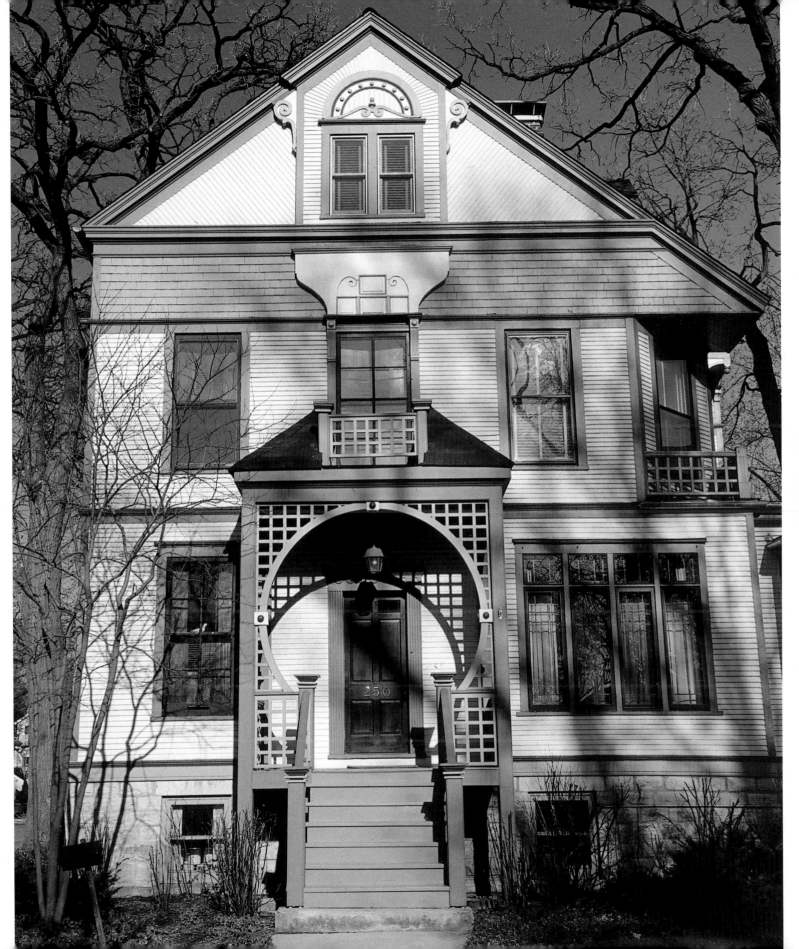

These apartment buildings, at 860 - 880 Lake Shore Drive in Chicago, were built by the German-born architect Ludwig Mies van der Rohe in 1948. Mies van der Rohe, once a director of the German Bauhaus school, designed in what was known as the International Style, creating functional but elegant buildings of brick, steel and glass.

Outdoor spaces

Living rooms

This Chicago home (above and right) is characterized by the powerful contrast of textures and lines, rough, exposed brick, ceiling beams along with pipes and smooth, clean surfaces of glass, wood and metal in the furniture and fittings.

This loft (top-left) has an area of 2,200 sq. ft., initially just bare walls and the mushroom shaped columns with walls, columns, floor and ceilings all made of

This residential loft designed by Ruhl Walker (above) was created in an 1,800 square foot shaft of space enlivened only by windows at both narrow ends but with spectacular morning and afternoon light and dramatic views of the Boston skyline.

This loft (right) by architect Sandy Jimenez maintains a large simple rectangle space with the original beams and exposed, refurbiched brick. Kitchen and bedroom have a plaster ceiling distinguishing it from the rest the space.

Here a former warehouse (left) was converted into six housing units. A 15-foot wide courtyard was created on the south side by removing roofing. The new facade for housing units along the length of the building gives onto the courtyard.

These housing units (right-bellow) are of two stories, with double height living spaces facing the courtyard. Furnishings combine modern and traditional concepts of design.

In this dwelling, designed by Ruhl Walker (left), the long windowless side walls have ceiling planes and custom millwork on one side and steel and back-lit acrylic on the other. The translucent wall is the primary light source for the entire loft, glowing with morning sunlight and evening built-in halogen light.

Lofts like this one (left) designed by Moneo Brock Studio, offer new possibilities in apartment living. Large, open spaces and high ceilings offer an ample scope for the vision of both architect and client.

Design for this house (left) by Moneo Brock Studio took advantage of the original posts of white oak and beams of yellow pine as well as the openness and fluidity of the space, accentuating that feeling by opening the roof at strategic points.

Jennifer Randall designed this Seattle home (left) in which high-tech elements blend with wood floors and classic furniture to create an environment that is both warm and original.

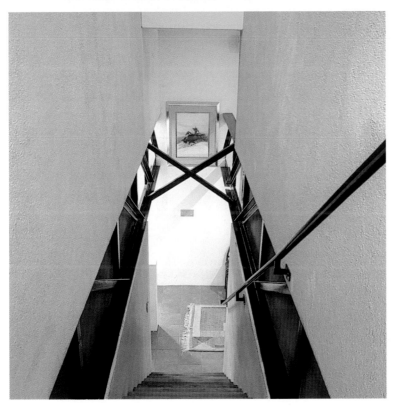

A folding aluminum stair provides access to the door leading to the roof deck. The stair is rigged to a counterweight and can be easily lifted overhead to open up the floor space.

Dinning rooms

This New York residence is the result of the renovation of a prewar apartment with 1,400 square feet of floor space, accentuating the massive, 20-inch thick exposed brick walls that extend the full depth of the apartment.

Kitchens

Razor sharp lines and geometrical volumes define the esthetic of this interior, designed by Hanraham & Meyers in which an ultra-modern simplicity creates an atmosphere that is both elegant and restful.

The kitchen (right), with a counter of Carrara marble, was also designed by the Moneo Brock studio, using the same clean, angular forms that occur in the rest of the apartment. Skylights and the use of color contribute to the warm, bright atmosphere.

Bathrooms